Jean Gilder Picture Book

by Jean Gilder

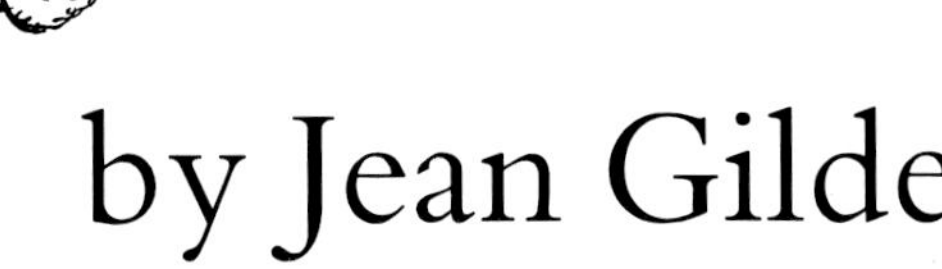

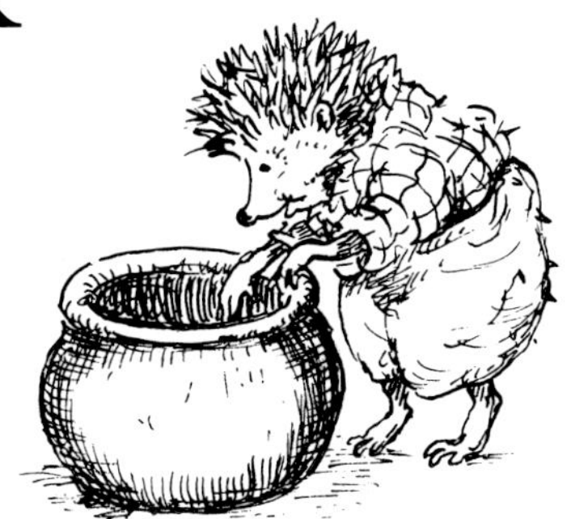

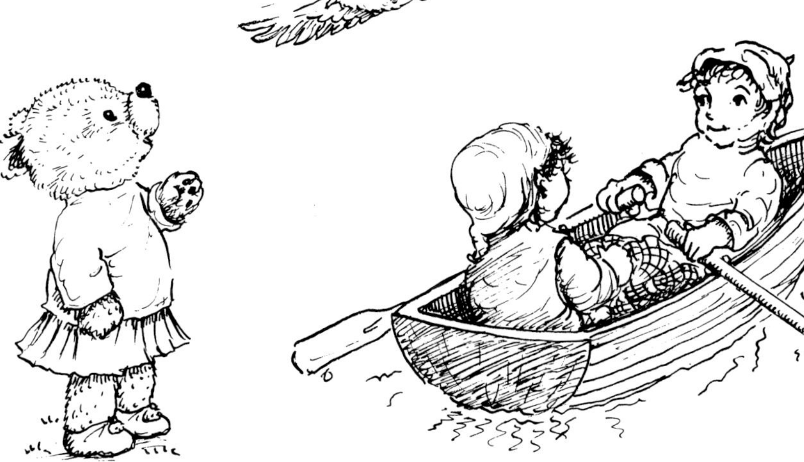

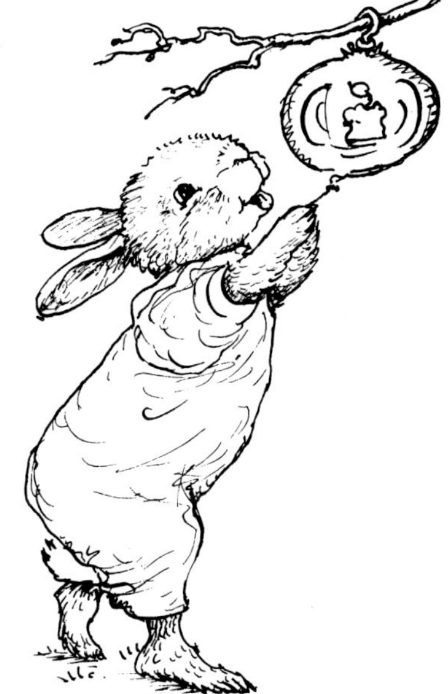

 Printed in England. B144 ISBN 0 85503 144 1

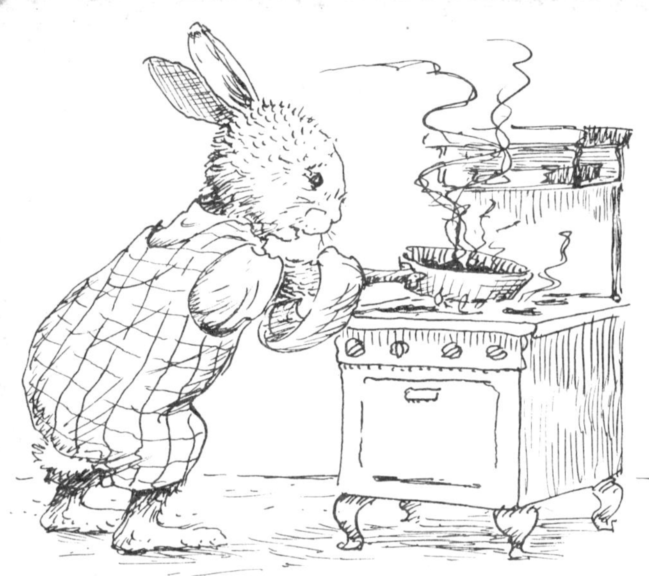

JOEY RABBIT MEETS THE GYPSIES

Joey Rabbit was tired. He had burnt his supper, and Mrs Bundle's babies were making a frightful noise next door.

With a sigh, he decided to go for a walk, and slammed the door behind him. As he walked through the woods, the sound of strange music and a delicious smell of cooking enticed him from the path! Through the bushes he saw a brightly painted caravan, and gypsy rabbits playing music and dancing while a huge pot bubbled over the fire.

As he edged closer, the gypsy rabbits heard the rustle of leaves, and froze. Joey stepped forward rather nervously. 'Er, er, I'm Joey! I love your music – and is that really braised turnip and herb dumpling stew in that pot ?'

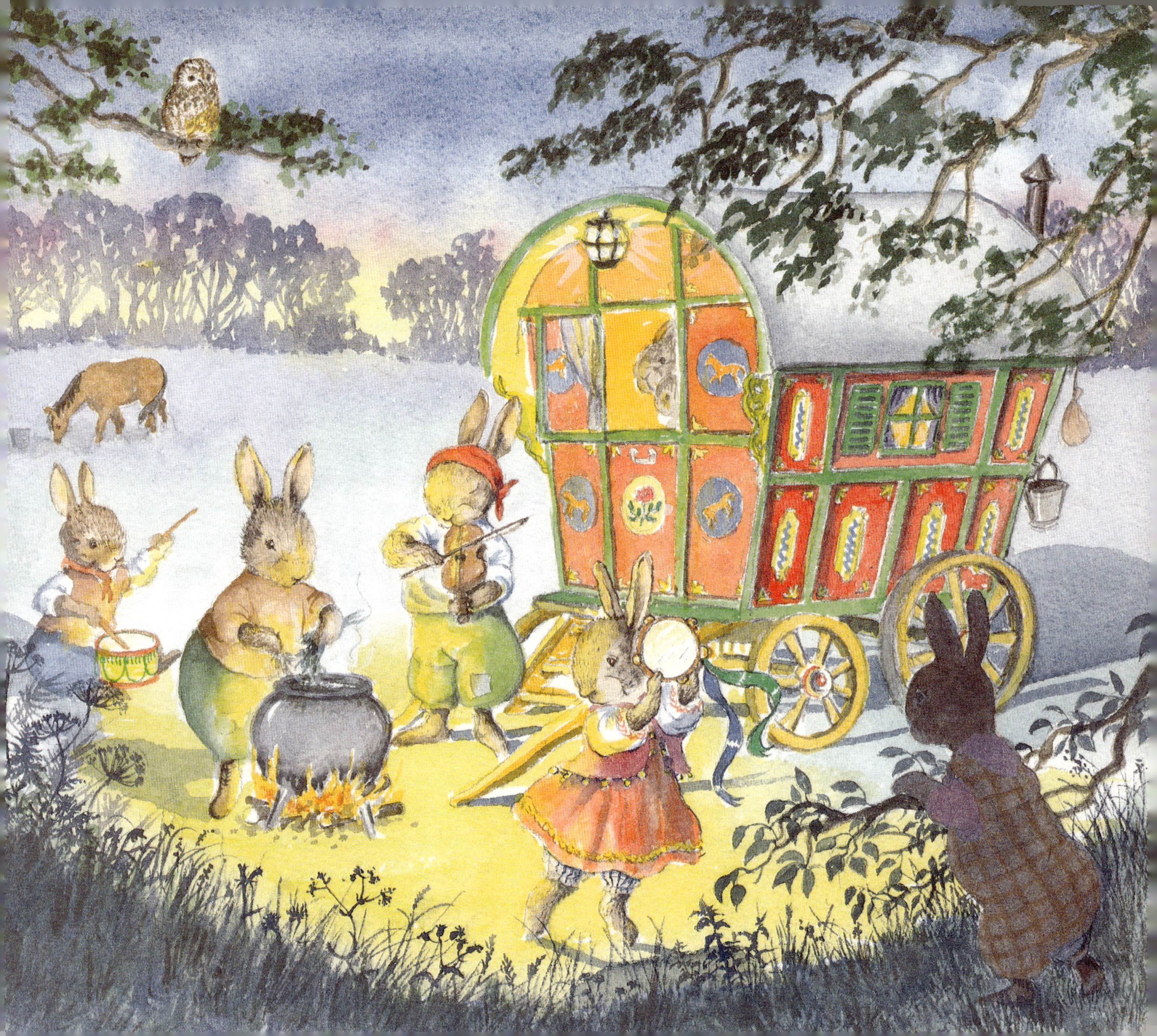

‘Why, It’s a village rabbit’ cried the fiddler with relief. ‘Welcome to our camp. Come and warm yourself, supper is nearly ready.’

Joey had a wonderful evening. The rabbits told him tales of far away places, and taught him their Gypsy dances.

But at last the owls flew home, and the moon set; and Joey began to think of his own little burrow; so after many good-byes and one last dance, Joey walked happily home to bed.

The next day, Joey took his friends to meet the Gypsies. But they had gone! ‘You must have been dreaming!’ they teased. But there was a circle of embers and tracks of the caravan wheels. ‘No’ said Joey, ‘It wasn’t a dream, and one day, they will return!’

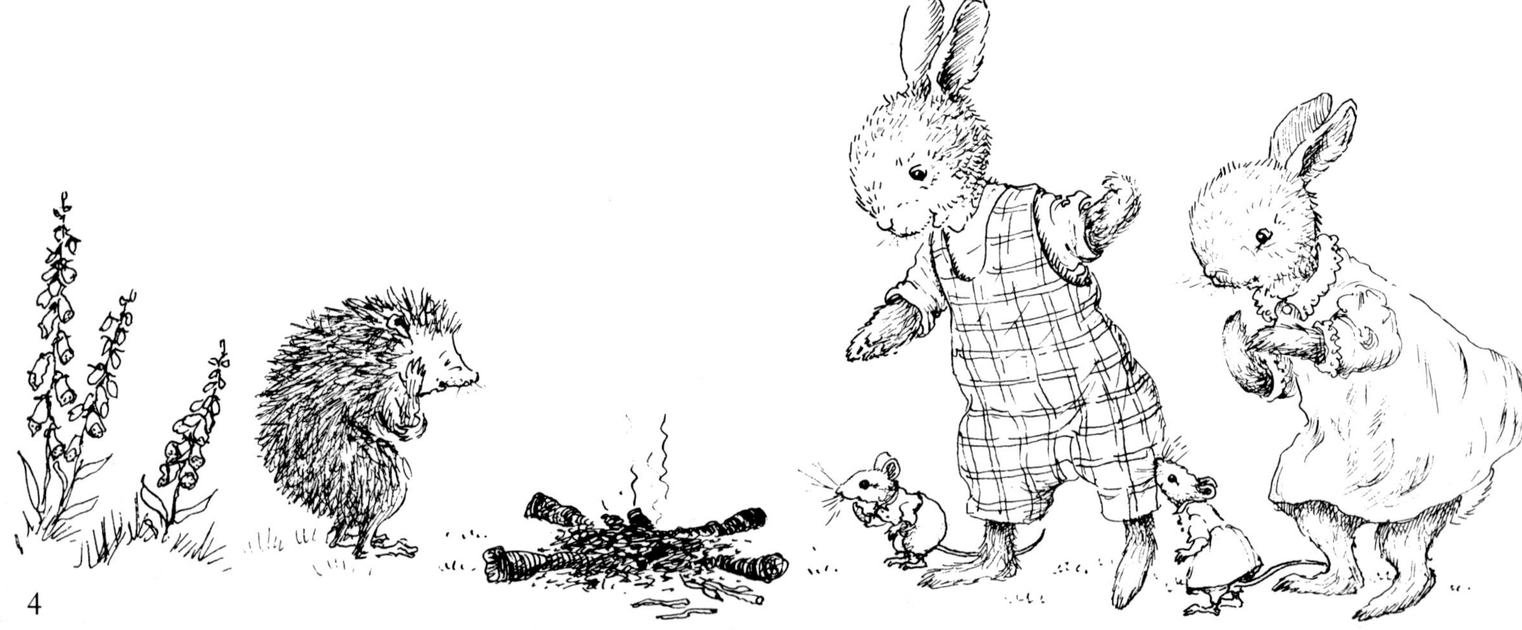

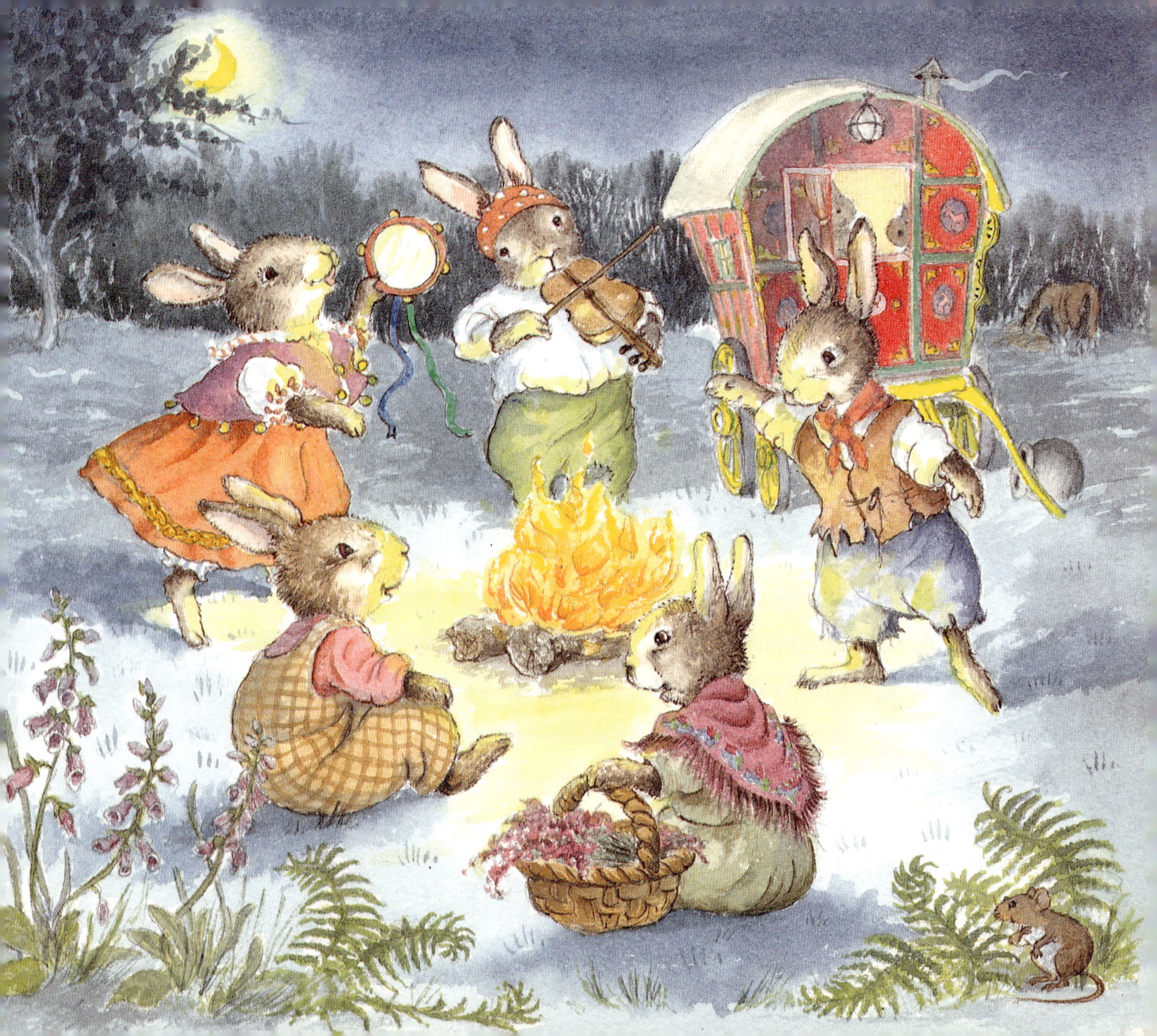

THE JUMBLE BIRTHDAY

Pansy Rabbit rummaged through her drawers and wardrobe, looking for a dress to wear for her bithday party. Soon she had a pile of old clothes. 'Not a single pretty dress to wear!' she muttered in annoyance. Her friend Daisy was passing. 'Let's hold a Jumble Sale,' she said. So the two friends set up stalls and arranged all the old clothes, books and toys that they had finished with. The woodland folk thought it was great fun trying on hats and dresses. They bought some very good bargains – and soon Daisy and Pansy had enough money for a new dress each.

The next day all their friends came back for the birthday party in the garden – all wearing a 'good bargain'!

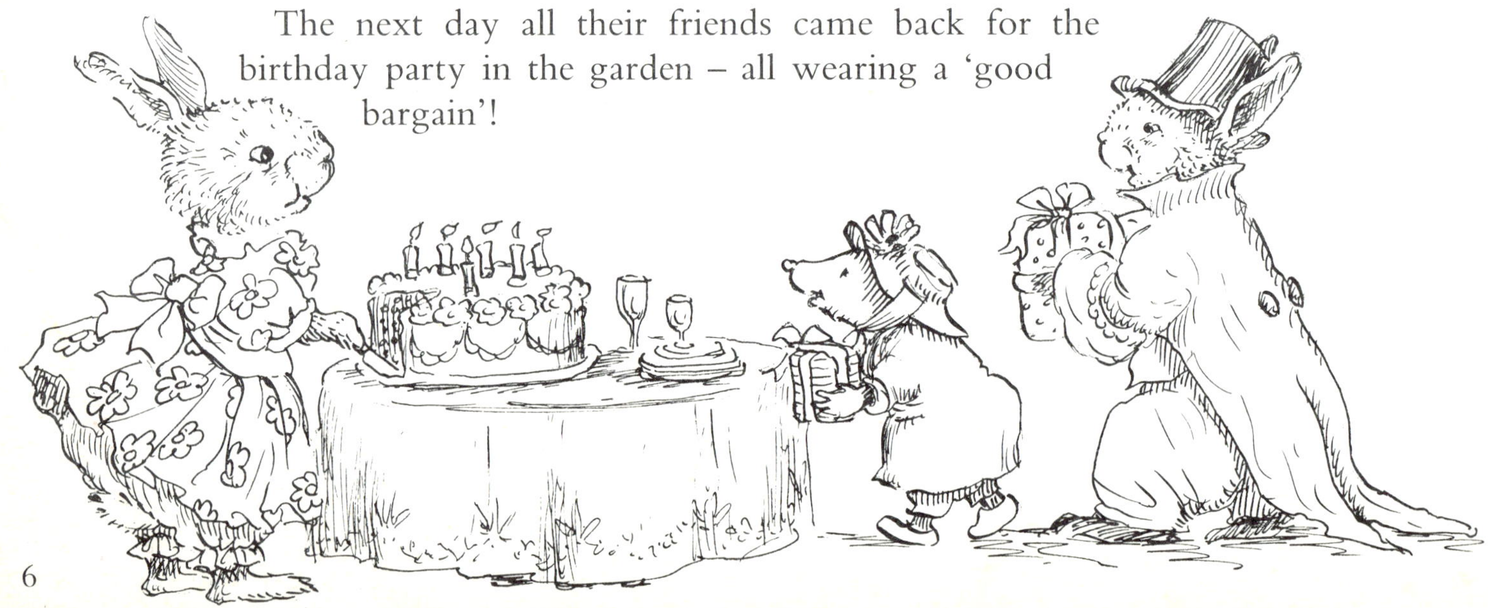

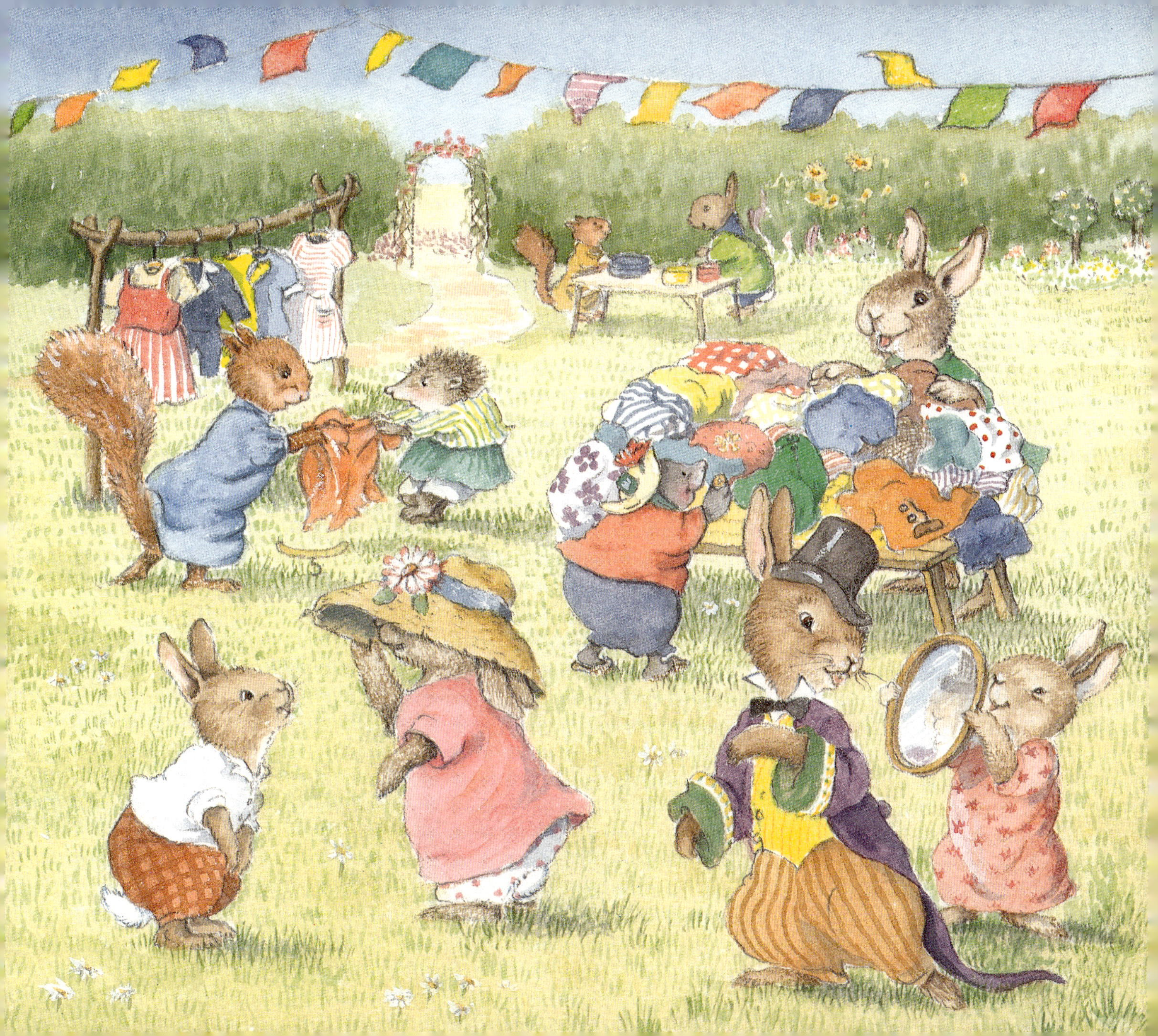

THE LAMPLIGHTER

Rufus Rabbit lived in a village called Deephollow.

It was rather a dusky place, full of dark corners in the evenings; so the woodland animals used to go to bed very early.

One day, Rufus was idly poking Jenny Hedgehog with a stick. She curled up tight and hoped he would go away.

'Now then, Rufus, what are you doing?' thundered a stern voice. Rufus looked up guiltily to see Mr Badger frowning at him.

'Nuffin', really,' stammered Rufus, 'It's just, well, I don't know what to do!'

Mr Badger thought for a while, then sat down with Rufus, and told him about his plan.

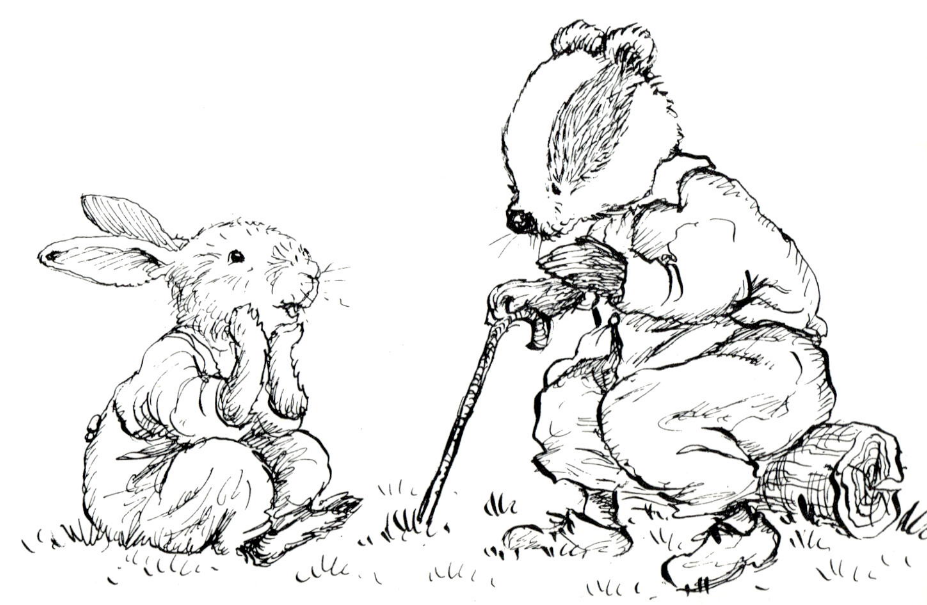

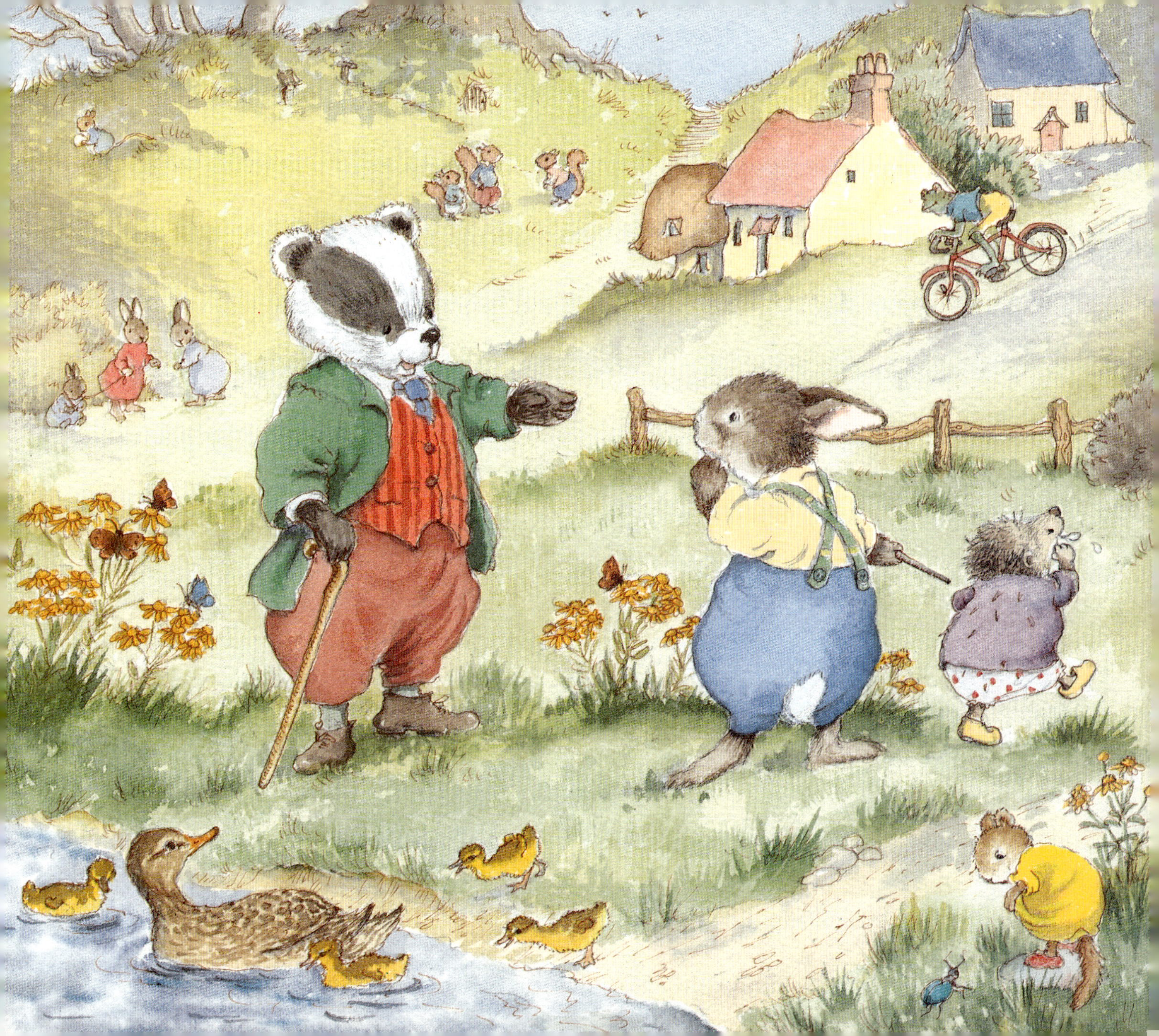

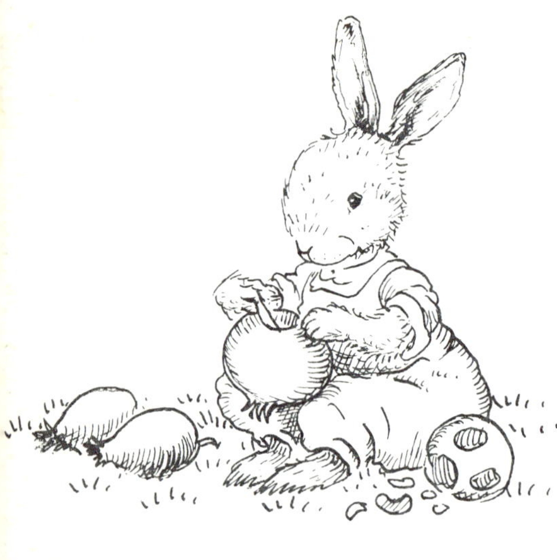

The next day, Rufus was seen busily hurrying about, collecting string, stout branches, and candles, while Mr Badger gave him directions. Then he hollowed out several rose hips.

That evening the folk of Deephollow had a wonderful surprise. As it grew dusk, Rufus rabbit hurried round, lighting all the lamps he had made. How pretty it was!

Rufus's friends were so pleased, as they could stay up late to play, and everyone said how clever he was. 'It was Mr Badger's idea,' said Rufus modestly.

But Rufus was delighted with his important new job, and never had time to be naughty again!

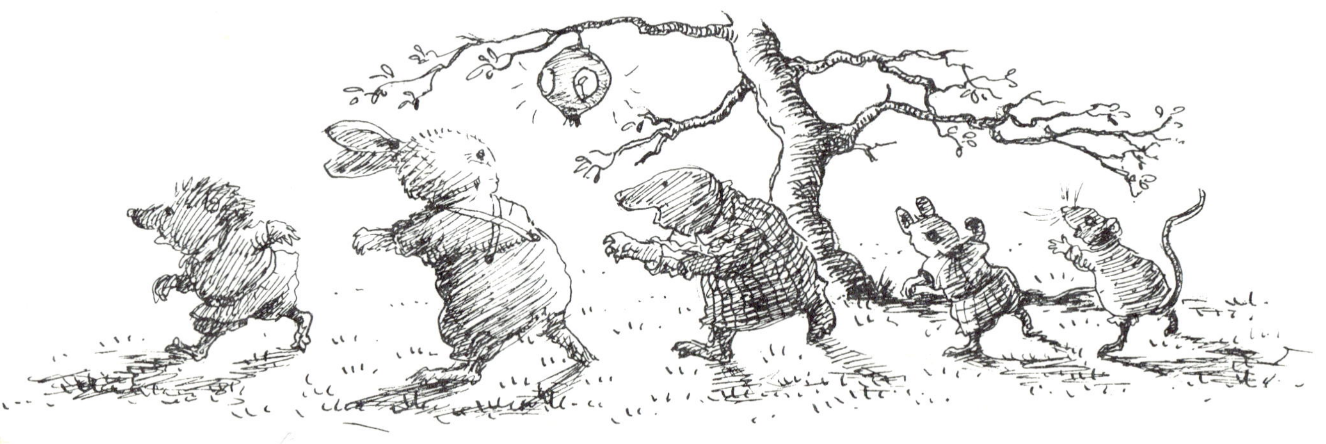

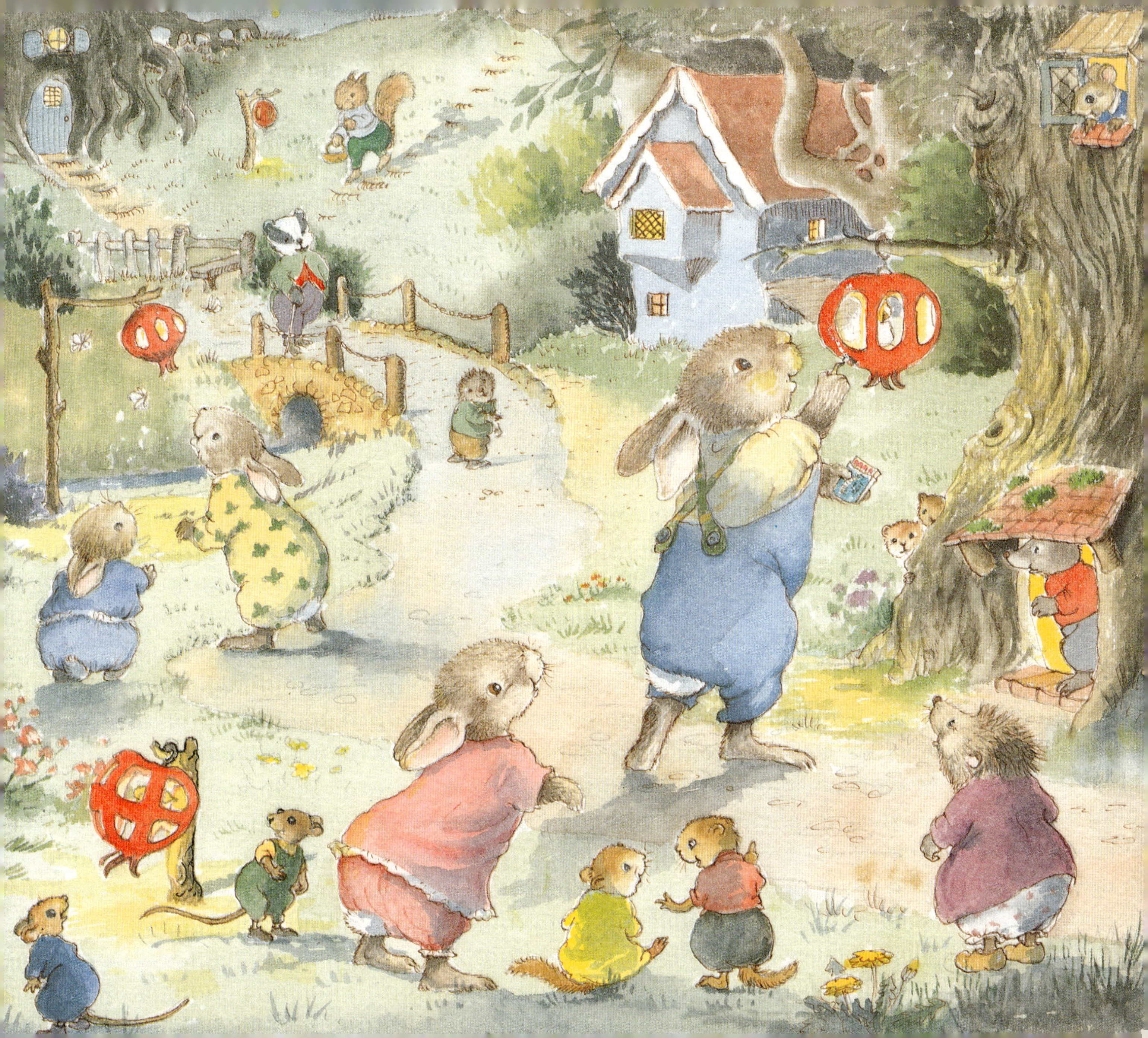

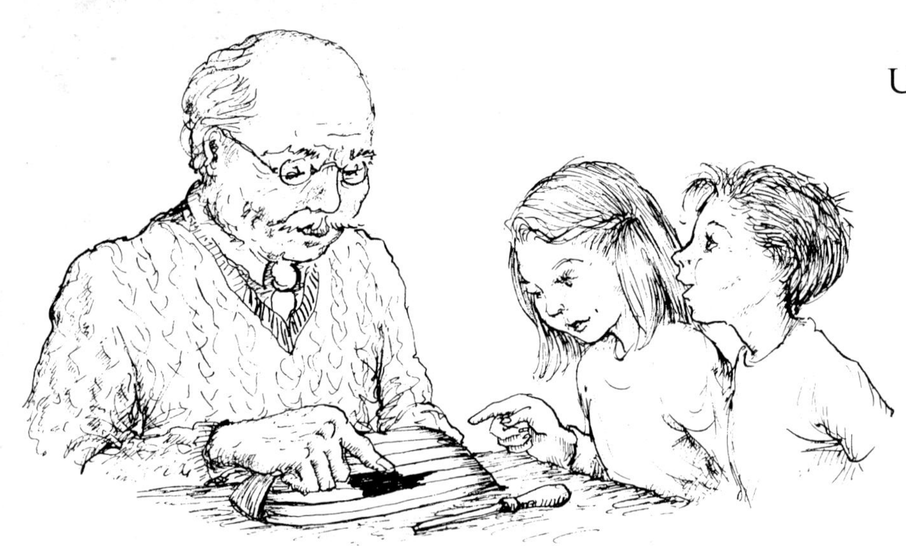

UNDER THE OAK TREE

When Margaret and Peter stayed with their Grandparents, they loved to play near the little stream at the bottom of the garden. One day, they found a tiny boat with a hole in the side. They took it to Grandfather, who carefully mended it.

'I should put it back, – it may belong to someone!' twinkled Gran'pa. The following evening, the children heard voices by the stream. They were amazed to see two little gnomes excitedly loading fishing nets into the boat by the light of a tiny lantern.

The next morning, there was a beautiful trout on the doorstep, wrapped in oakleaves.

'That is the gnomes' way of saying "Thank you" ' remarked Grandmother, 'They are very pleased to have their boat back!'

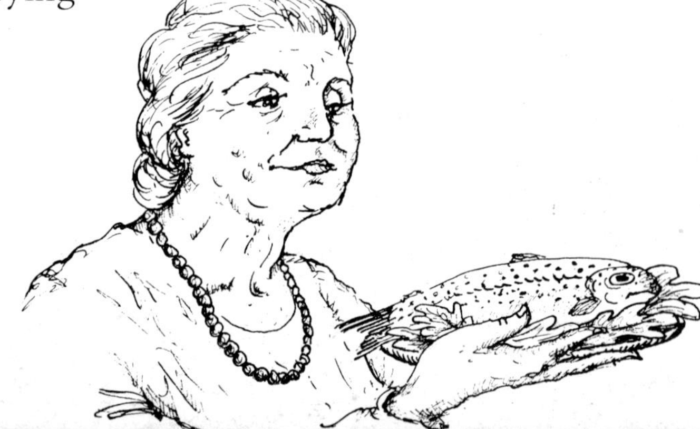

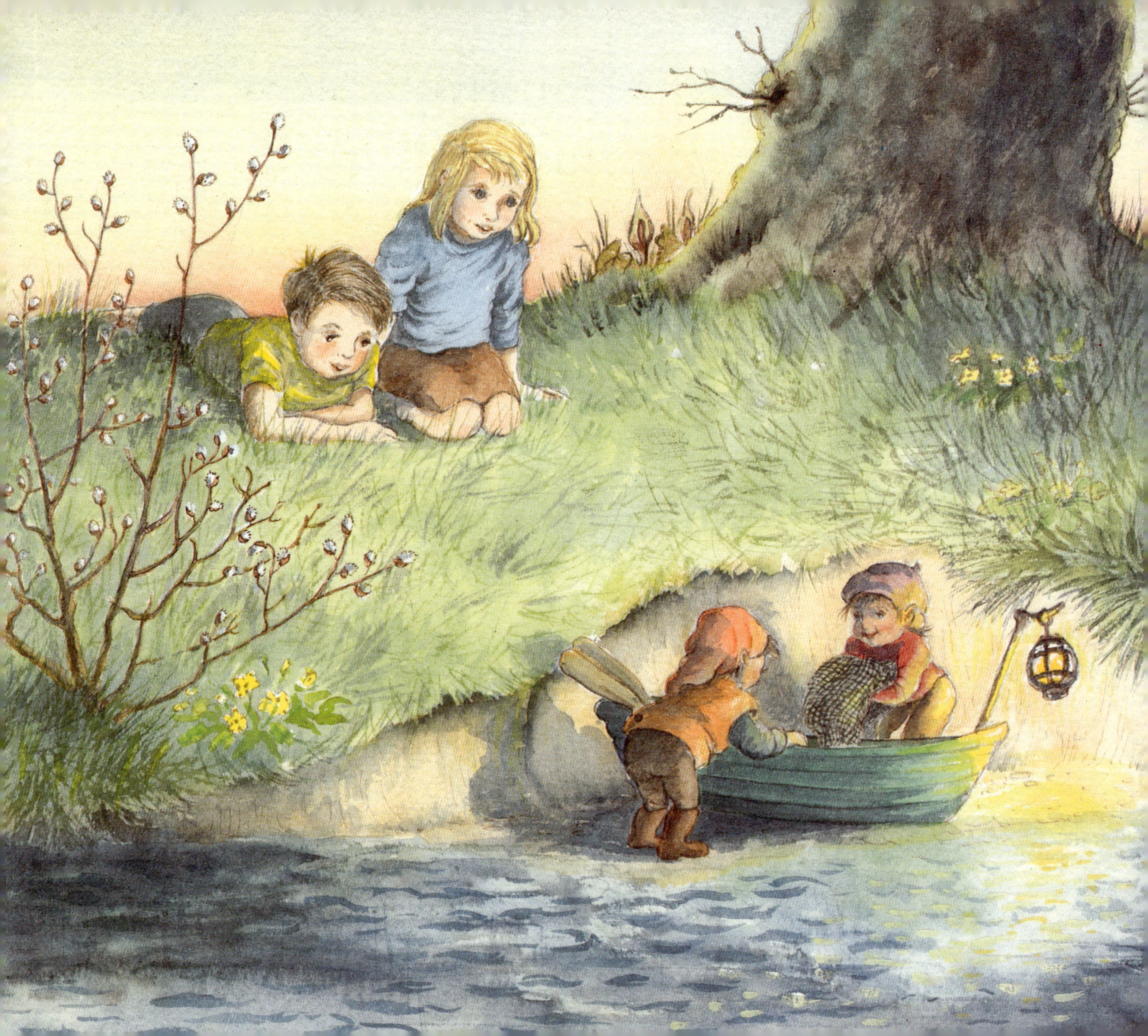

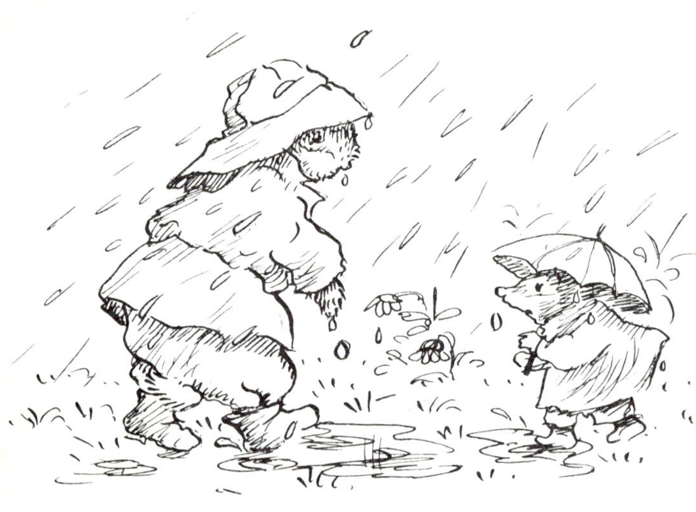

MRS BUNNY'S BAKING DAY

The young Bunnies were home for the school holidays. Usually they loved to play outside, but today it was raining.

'Oh, it's so boring when it rains!' they grumbled.

Mrs Bunny said she had to do some baking, so Granny suggested they all made some cakes.

They did enjoy themselves! It was rather messy, with jam, sugar and flour scattered freely; But soon, a smell of baking filled the air, and in no time there were jam tarts, cherry cake, iced cakes and apple pie on the table.

After that, the sun came out, and the rabbits went out to play.

'I liked this baking day,' remarked Ben Bunny, 'I hope it rains again tomorrow!'

'I hope NOT,' laughed Mummy 'we already have enough cakes for a week!'

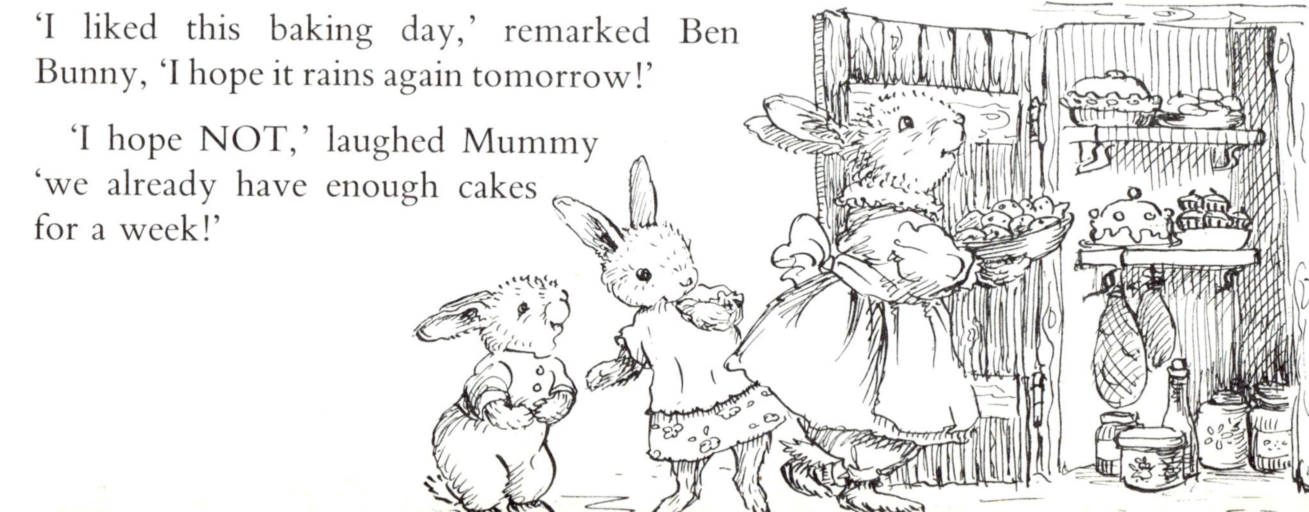

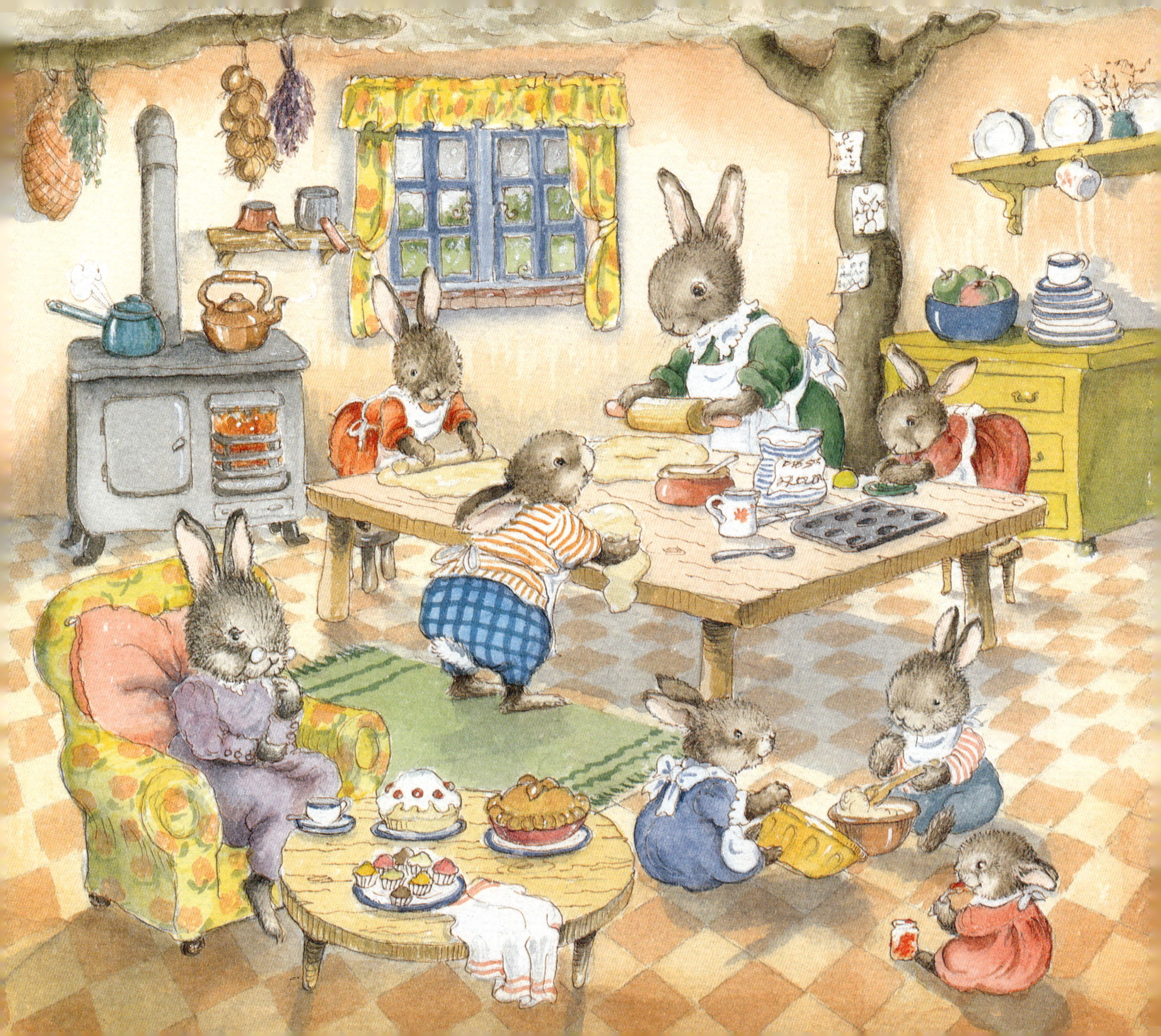

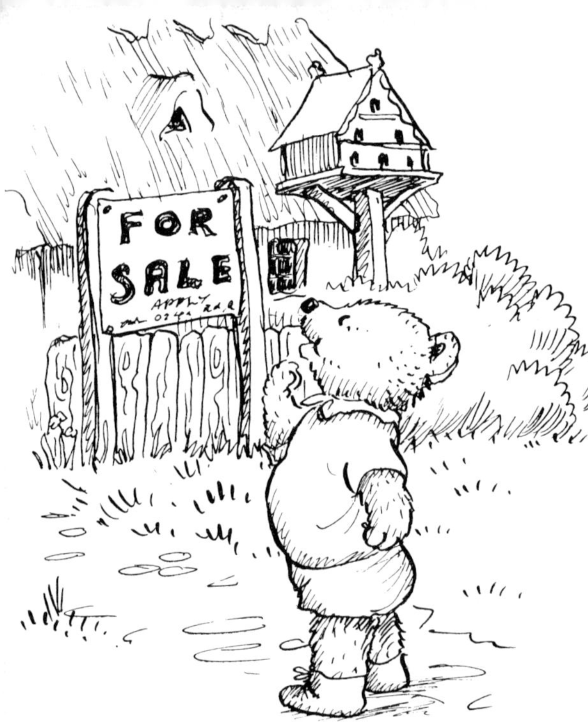

TEDDY'S MOVING DAY

The Teddies lived in a tiny house. 'No room for anything,' said Mummy Bear crossly, 'I even have to do the washing-up outside!'

Daddy Bear soon found a cottage for sale, and decided to buy it. 'It's very pretty,' he told his family, 'and has white doves living in the garden'.

'We must think of a name for the cottage,' said Mummy Bear excitedly.

At last moving day came, and the furniture was packed onto the cart.

When the Bears arrived at the cottage, the white doves were very pleased to see them. Mummy bear gave them some corn to eat.

'Let's call our new house "Dove Cottage",' said Daddy Bear. So they were very happy there.

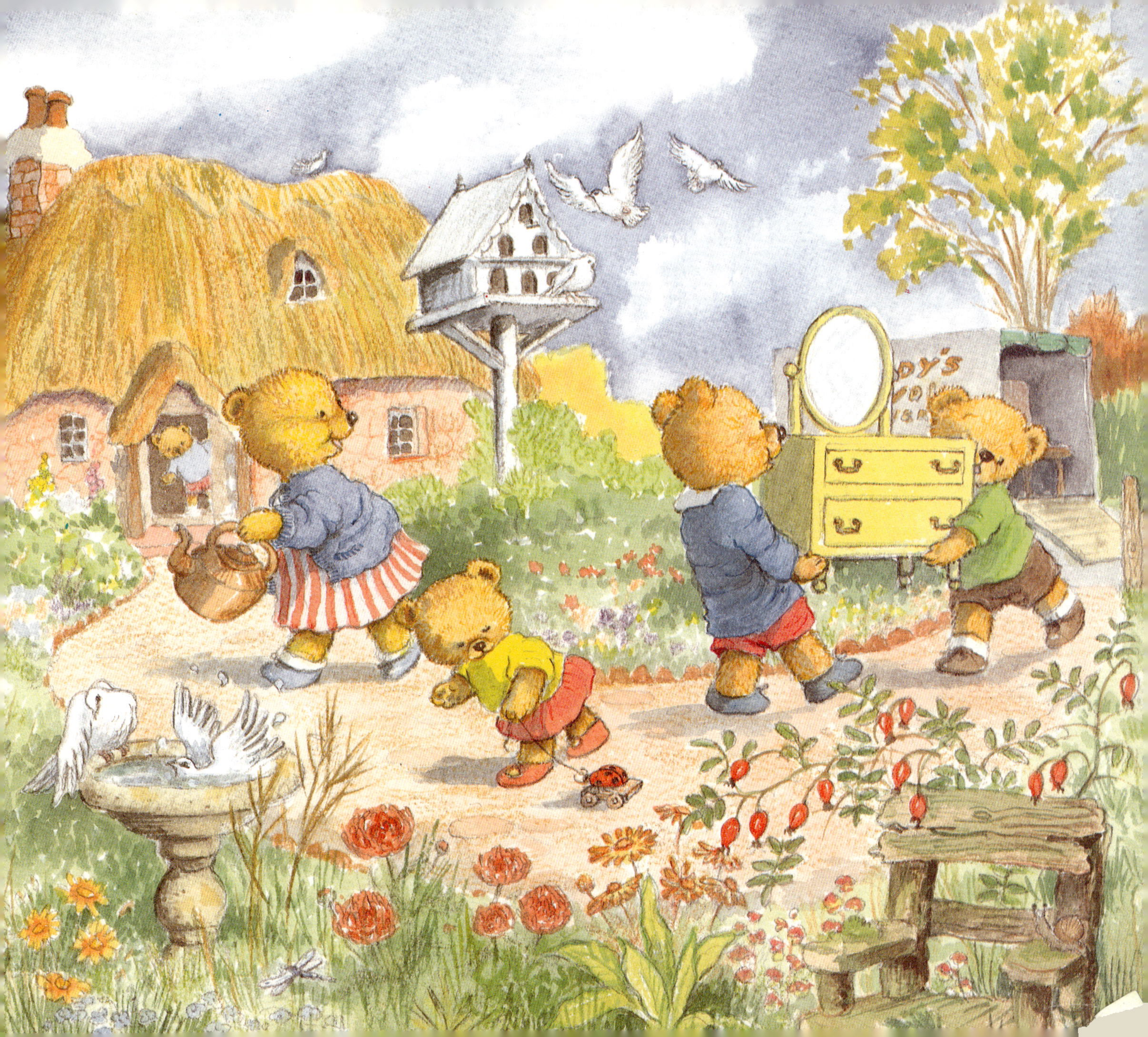

THE SHOP IN THE WOODS

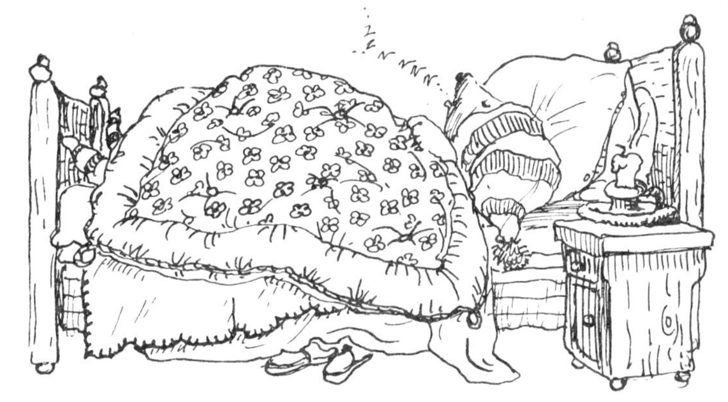

As Christmas Eve drew near, Mrs Mole knew she couldn't carry on. After a nasty cold she was tired and needed a rest from running the village shop: so she closed up and went to have a long sleep in her cosy bed.

Later, Postman Badger expressed his worries to Biddy Bunny. 'No sign of Mrs Mole – no lights on, curtains drawn, and the shop closed for two days,' he told her. 'We must go at once and see if she's all right,' exclaimed Biddy.

Mrs Mole yawned as she opened the door to Biddy and Badger. 'I'm not ill,' she explained, 'I was just very tired !' Soon all her friends came to help: dusting, tidying and bringing cakes, nuts and biscuits from the store rooms. When Mrs Mole opened the shop she was very busy indeed, but smiled to herself as she thought of her kind friends.

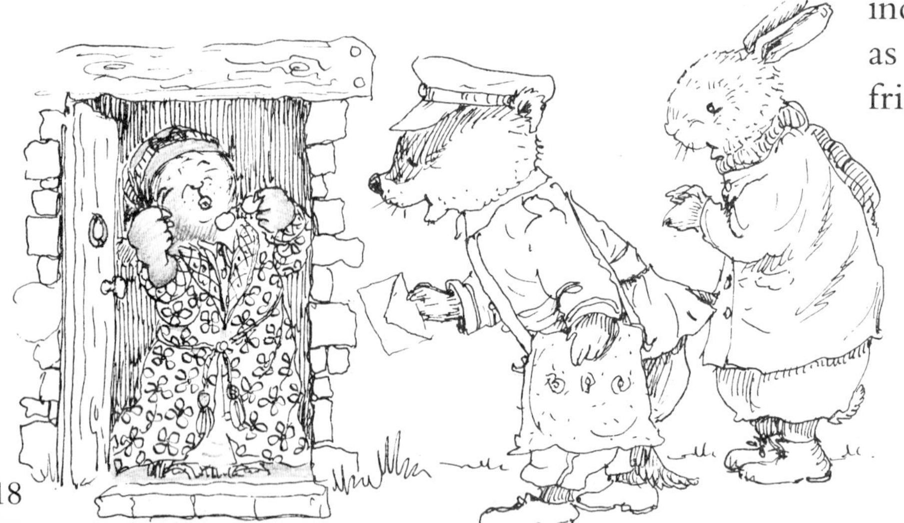

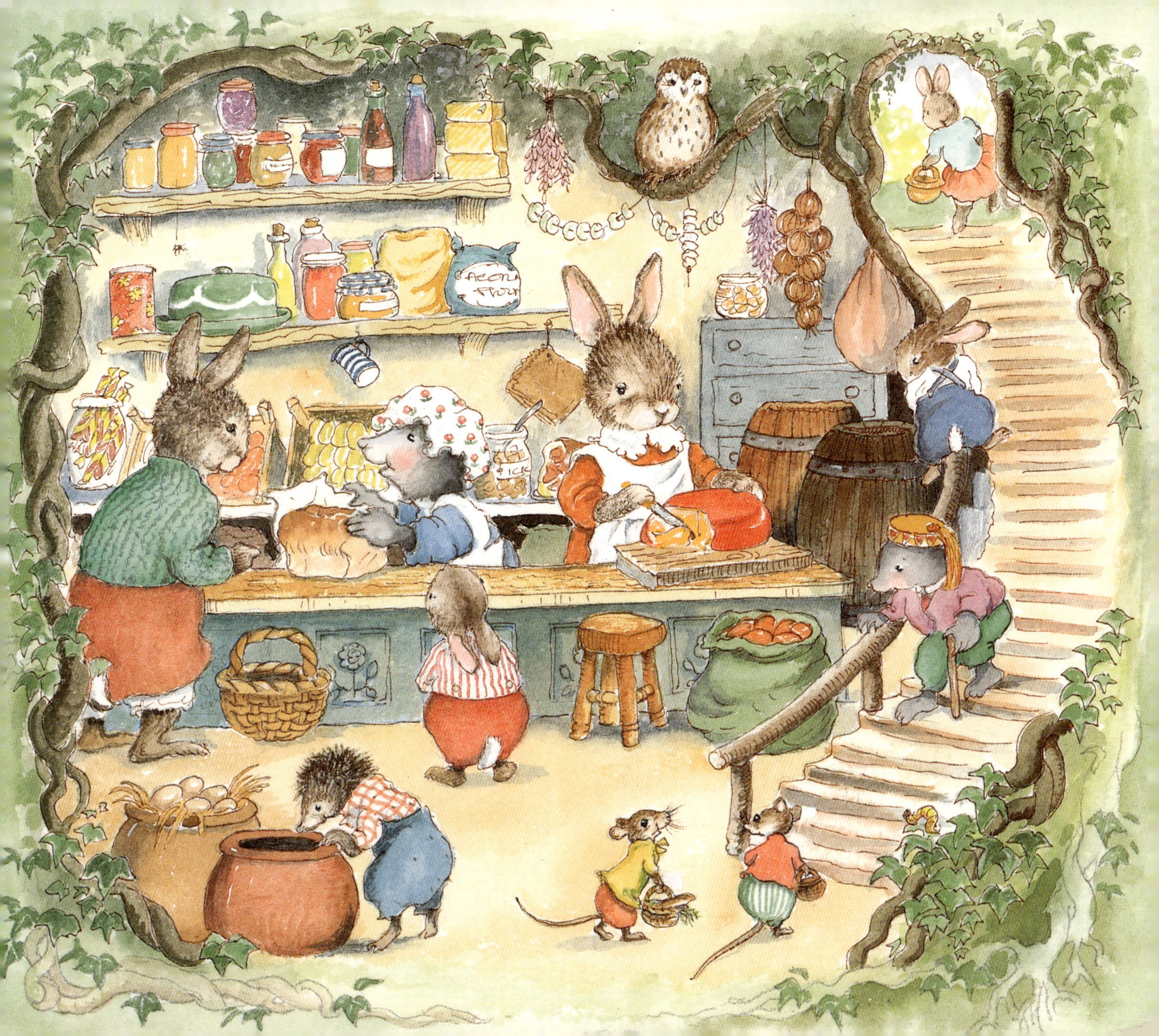

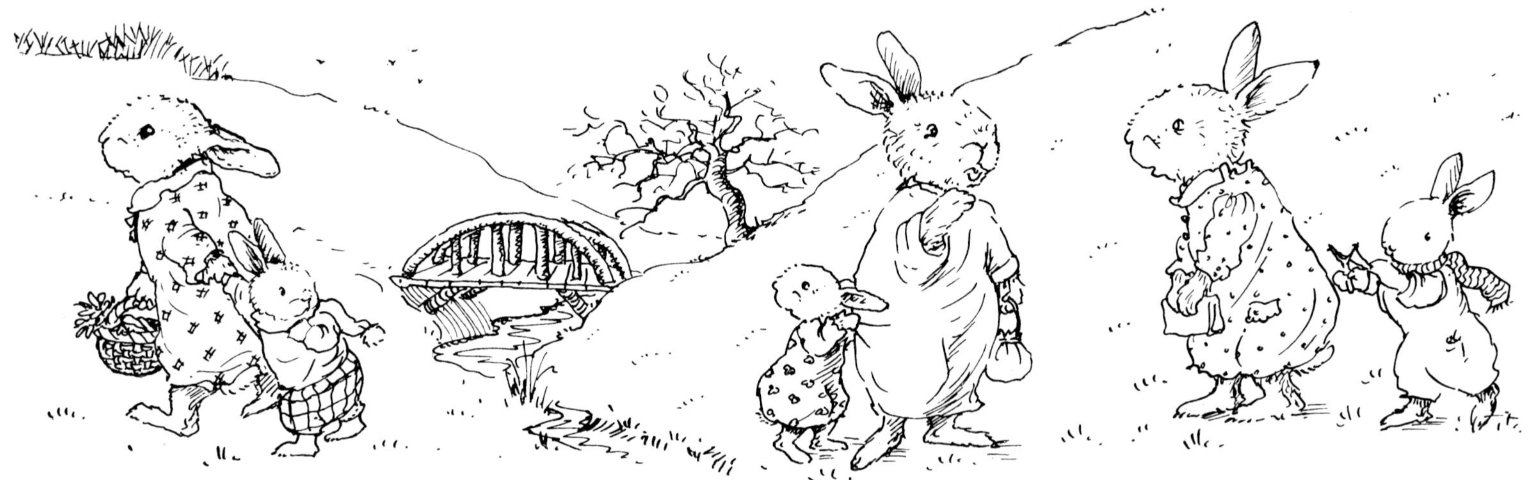

SNOW IN DANDELION DELL

The rabbits who lived on the lower side of the stream that divided Dandelion Dell did not like the rabbits who lived on the higher side of the hill. That was silly, because nobody could quite remember the long ago quarrel which had caused this.

But one winter's day, everything changed! The rabbits awoke to a white, still world of snow and ice.

'Oh, can we go out and play?' asked the youngest rabbits; Soon, they were snowballing each other across the stream, and having such fun that they all crossed the bridge backwards and forwards, and were laughing and shaking paws – and the silly quarrel was quite forgotton for ever!

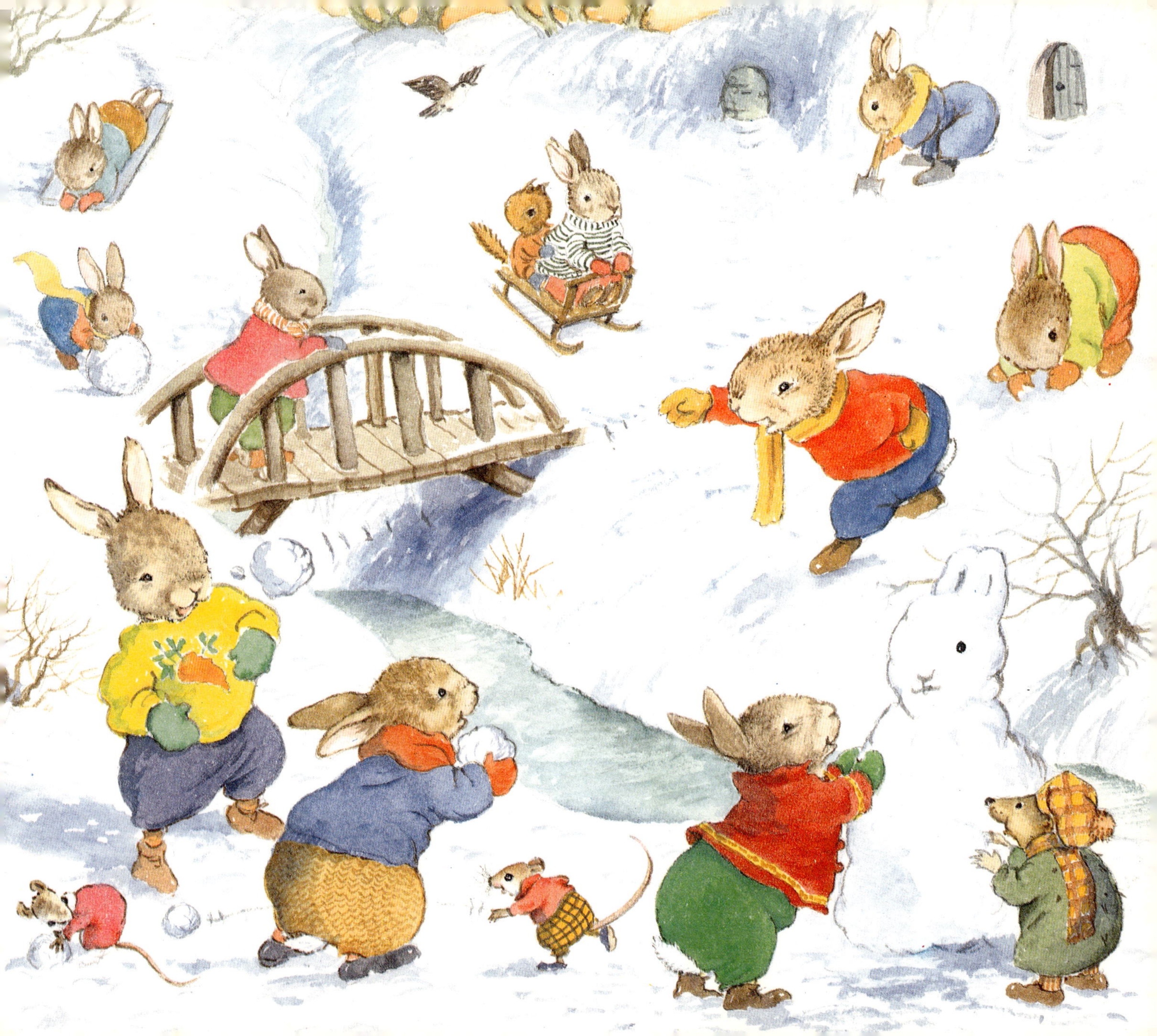

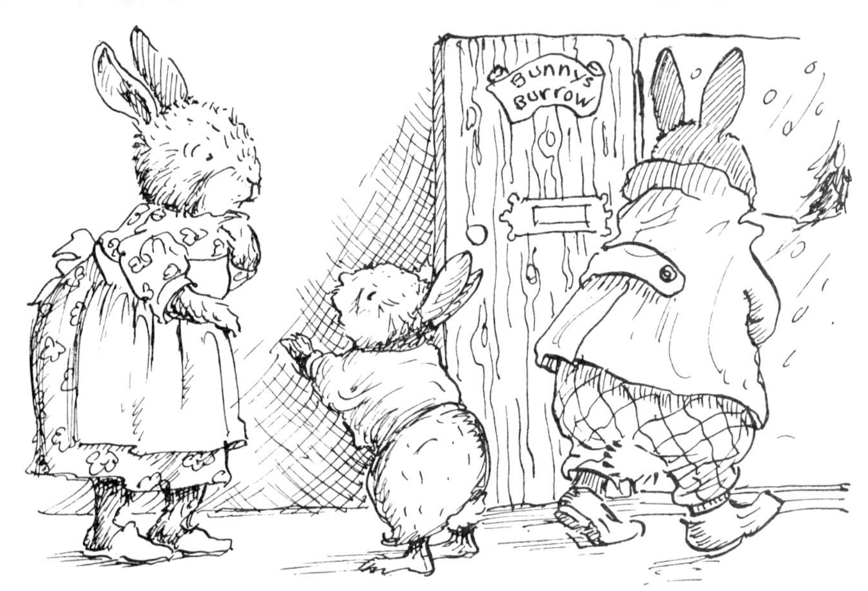

THE BIGGEST CHRISTMAS TREE

Billy Bunny knew Christmas was coming. He was very excited – Christmas meant parties, Christmas trees, and Presents!

'But Mummy, how can we get a BIG Christmas tree into our burrow?' puzzled Billy. 'Well, you can have a party, anyway,' said his Mummy, kindly.

On the day of the party, Billy woke to a white, snowy world. He wanted to go out and play, but he had to help his Mummy to get ready for the party. Daddy Bunny went out, looking mysterious.

When the time came for the party – no-one had arrived. Billy was nearly in tears. 'Where are my friends?' he asked.

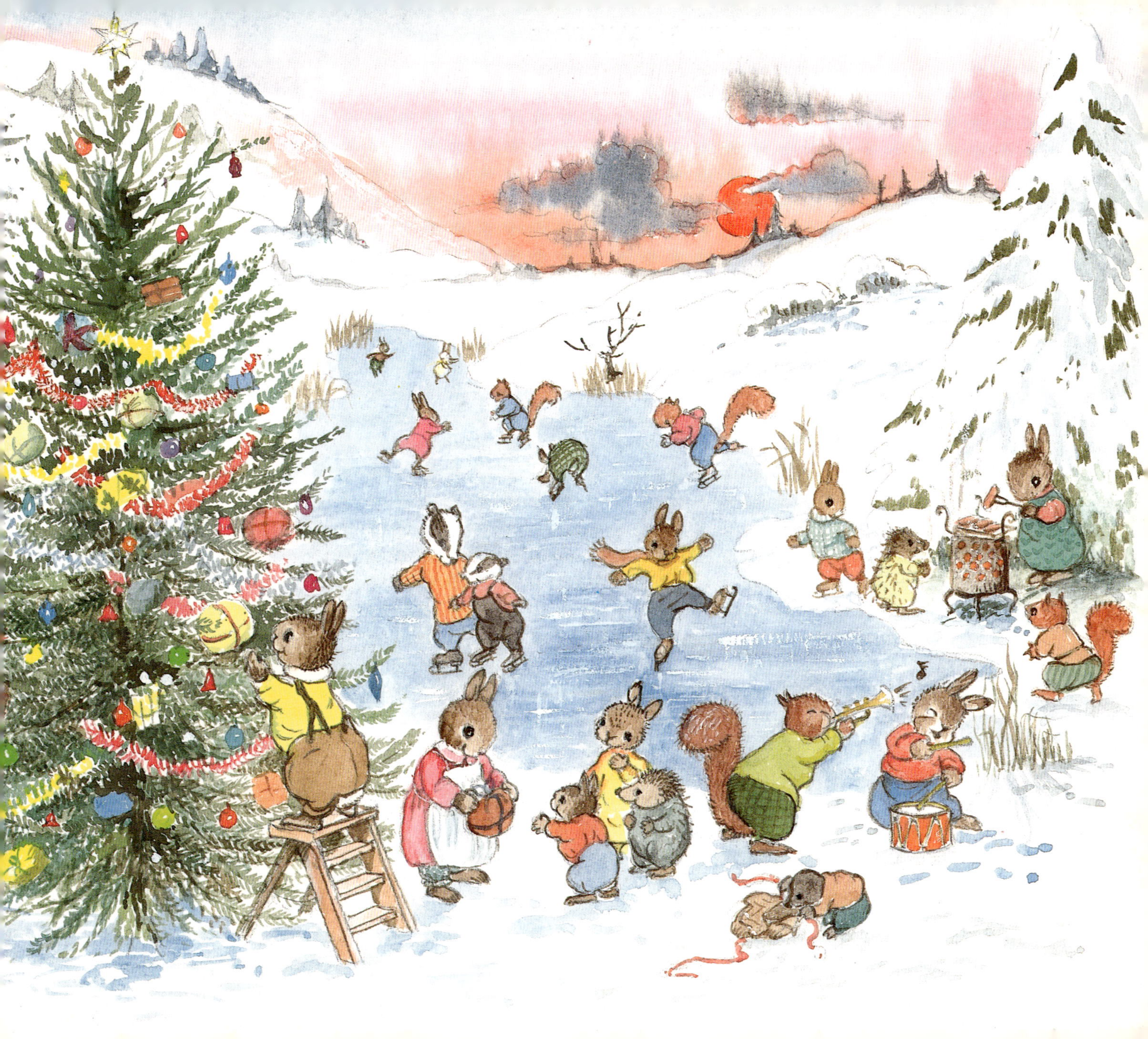

'Coat and gloves on, and come and see!' said his Daddy cheerfully.

They took Billy down to the big pond which was frozen over. Beside the pond was a huge Christmas tree, beautifully decorated and hung with presents for everybody; and all his friends were waiting for him.

What fun they had! They skated on the ice and played games in the snow and Aunt Fluff cooked sausages over a hot fire. After that they all picked their presents from the tree. Then, as the sun set, the animals went home for mince pies and hot apple tea.

'What a lovely time,' sighed Billy, 'And it was the BIGGEST Christmas tree I've ever seen!'

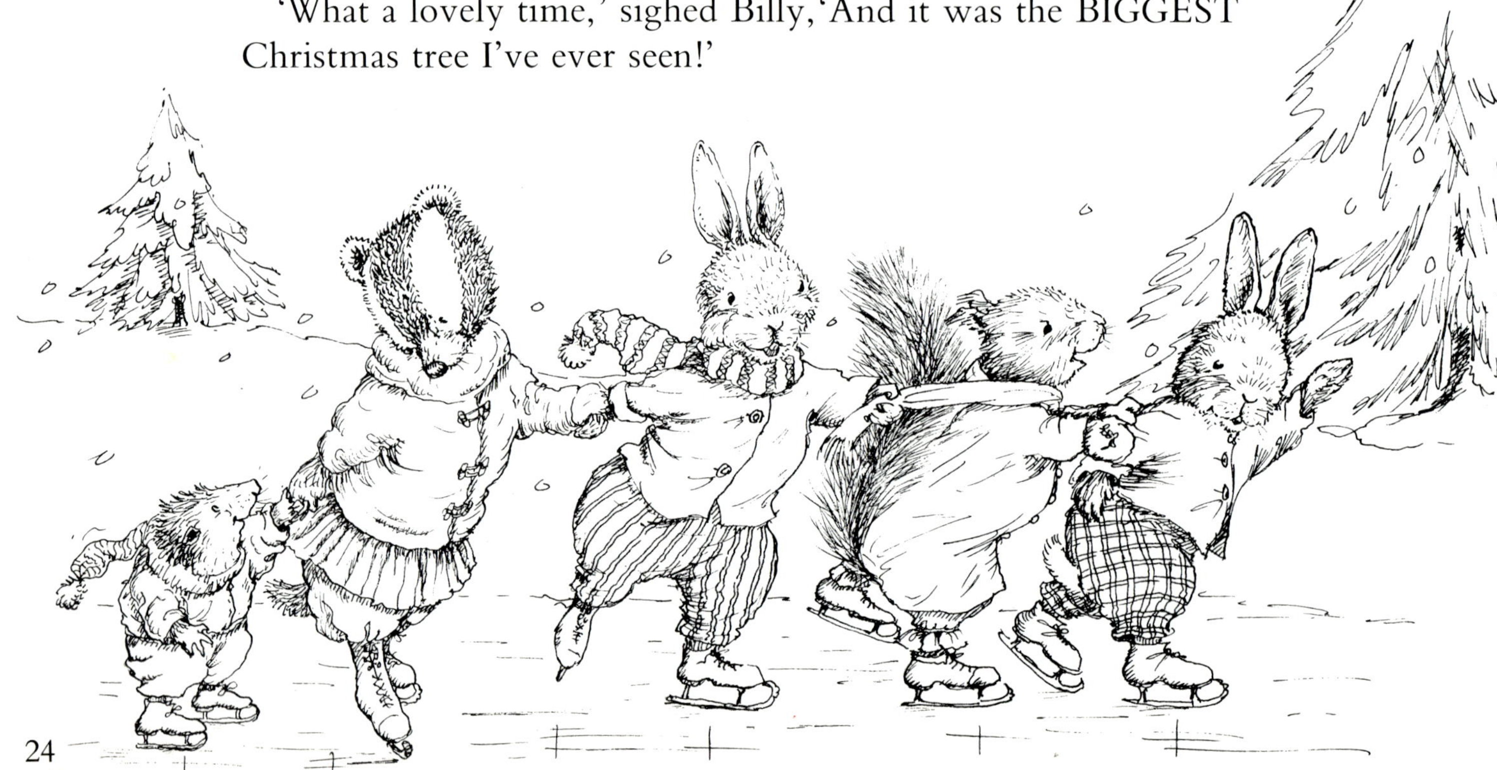